ROSALIND AND JACK JANSSEN

EGYPTIAN
HOUSEHOLD ANIMALS

SHIRE EGYPTOLOGY

Cover illustration
Blue faience tile depicting a man leading a large hound.
From Malkata(?), West Thebes, Eighteenth Dynasty.
81 by 62 mm.
(R.116. Courtesy of the Nicholson Museum, University of Sydney.)

British Library Cataloguing in Publication Data:
Janssen, Rosalind.
Egyptian Household Animals.
1. Ancient Egypt, Pets.
I. Title. II. Janssen, Jack.
636.0887'0932.
ISBN 0-7478-0000-6.

Published by
SHIRE PUBLICATIONS LTD
Cromwell House, Church Street, Princes Risborough,
Aylesbury, Bucks HP17 9AJ, UK.

Series Editor: Barbara Adams

ISBN 0 7478 0000 6

First published 1989

Printed in Great Britain by
C. I. Thomas & Sons (Haverfordwest) Ltd,
Press Buildings, Merlins Bridge, Haverfordwest, Dyfed.

Contents

Acknowledgements

We wish to express our gratitude to the museum curators who have provided photographs, in many cases gratis, and permission for their publication. In particular, the cover illustration is reproduced by courtesy of the Nicholson Museum of the University of Sydney. Dr Günter Burkhard kindly supplied us with a photocopy of an obscure article.

Mr Peter Harrison and Mr Nicholas Moss of the Central Photographic Unit, University College London, have displayed their habitual aptitude in the photography of objects from the Petrie Museum, some of which were taken especially for this book. All are the copyright of the Department of Egyptology, University College of London. The line drawings are the painstaking work of Mrs Helena Jaeschke.

Acknowledgement is made to Professor W. J. Murnane and Penguin Books for permission to reproduce in abbreviated form the chronology on pages 5 and 6.

4

List of illustrations

Chronology

Predynastic and Protodynastic	before 3050 BC		
Early Dynastic or Archaic Period	3050-2613 BC		
		3050-2890	Dynasty I *Horus Aha*
		2890-2686	Dynasty II
		2686-2613	Dynasty III
Old Kingdom	2613-2181 BC		
		2613-2498	Dynasty IV
		2498-2345	Dynasty V
		2345-2181	Dynasty VI
First Intermediate Period	2181-2040 BC		
		2181-2040	Dynasties VII-X
		2134-2060	Dynasty XI (Theban)
		2117-2069	*Antef II*
Middle Kingdom	2040-1782 BC		
		2060-1991	Dynasty XI
		1991-1782	Dynasty XII
Second Intermediate Period	1782-1570 BC		
		1782-1650	Dynasties XIII and XIV (Egyptian)
		1663-1555	Dynasties XV and XVI (Hyksos)
		1663-1570	Dynasty XVII (Theban)

New Kingdom	1570-1070 BC		
		1570-1293	Dynasty XVIII
		1504-1450	*Tuthmosis III*
		1498-1483	*Hatshepsut*
		1453-1419	*Amenophis II*
		1386-1349	*Amenophis III*
		1350-1334	*Amenophis IV/Akhenaten*
		1321-1293	*Horemheb*
		1293-1185	Dynasty XIX
		1291-1278	*Seti I*
		1279-1212	*Ramesses II*
		1185-1070	Dynasty XX
		1182-1151	*Ramesses III*
		1141-1133	*Ramesses VI*

Third Intermediate Period	1070-713 BC		
		1070-945	Dynasty XXI
		945-712	Dynasty XXII
		828-712	Dynasty XXIII
		724-713	Dynasty XXIV

Late Period	713-332 BC		
		713-656	Dynasty XXV (Nubian)
			Tefnakhte of Sais
		664-525	Dynasty XXVI
		525-404	Dynasty XXVII (Persian)
		404-399	Dynasty XXVIII
		399-380	Dynasty XXIX
		380-343	Dynasty XXX (Egyptian/Persian)

Graeco-Roman	332 BC to AD 395		
		332-30	Ptolemies
		30 BC-AD 395	Roman Emperors

1
The relationship between men and animals

Modern man takes for granted the superiority expressed in the Old Testament story of the creation and his right to 'dominion over the fish of the sea, and over the fowl of the air, and over the cattle, and over all the earth, and over every living thing that moveth upon the earth'. The ancient Egyptians believed, however, that men and animals were together created by the god, as a hymn dedicated to the sun god Re testifies: 'Thou art the begetter who causes thy children to come into being: men, gods, flocks, herds, and all creeping animals.' They considered themselves, therefore, not so much lords of the beasts, but rather their interdependent partners (figure 1).

Hence the division between men and animals was less marked and their ties were stronger than those between people today and animals, except those with our pets. The Egyptians also owned pets, but beasts of burden and even wild and exotic creatures were equally regarded as partners, a relationship amply confirmed by both texts and representations. Animals were kept primarily to serve man, providing labour and sustenance or being slaughtered for food offerings, as a Middle Kingdom text exemplifies 'He [the god] has made for them [men] herbs, cattle, fowl and fish, to nourish them.' In addition, however, the beasts were both cherished and respected. From the earliest times the Egyptians were exhorted to care for their fellow creatures, as substantiated by an Old Kingdom *Pyramid Spell* stating that animals, on a par with humans, could accuse the king if he mistreated them. Indeed, the simile of the Pharaoh as herdsman of his people occurs long before the biblical motif of the 'Good Shepherd'. A unique, but unfortunately fragmentary, veterinary papyrus from the Middle Kingdom contains prescriptions for the treatment of the eyes of both a bull and a dog, indicative of the attentive care of sick animals. Schoolteachers frequently cited various animals as models of tractability when faced with their unruly and unteachable pupils.

Yet, probably more than in most civilisations, animals were loved as fellow creatures next in affection to a man's relatives and friends, although they were not, in general, accorded the holiness of, for example, cows in Hindu India. Frequent representations depict humans carrying young animals on their shoulders (figure

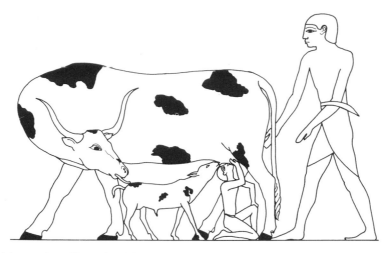

1. A boy and a calf together drinking from a cow. From the tomb of Baqt at Beni Hasan, Twelfth Dynasty. (After Rosellini, *Mon. Civ.*, 1834, plate XXVII.)

2). Significantly, out of over seven hundred hieroglyphic signs, nearly one-fifth represent mammals and birds or parts of them. Some quadrupeds, notably dogs and horses, were given human names, indicating that their owners attributed personalities to them. Conversely, men and women bore animal names, such as 'The Dog', 'The (Tom) Cat', 'The Foal', 'The Kid' or 'The Goose'.

Thus, although the gulf between men and animals was narrower in ancient Egypt than in modern experience, the difference is not so large that many similarities cannot be recognised from contemporary life.

2. Men bringing animals and fowl. From the mastaba of Seshethotep at Giza, Fifth Dynasty. (After Junker, *Giza*, II, 1934, figure 31.)

2
Dogs

Dogs originate from the wolf as their similar barking mechanisms attest. Jackals are also sometimes regarded as their progenitors although they have a completely different vocalisation pattern. The Egyptians did not always differentiate between dogs and jackals, sometimes even using the same word for both canines. One word for dog is the onomatopoeic *iuiu* ('barker', 'howler'). As the earliest domesticated creatures, dogs appear in association with man from early prehistory onwards, when they roamed around the settlements and were used for hunting.

During Egyptian history several breeds developed although the diversity was not nearly so great as in modern times. Some forms were clearly products of selective breeding, especially the greyhound type of the Old Kingdom, which is similar to the modern basenji from Central Africa, with its erect pointed ears and curly tail. This is the ideal specimen which occurs frequently in representations, though it may be doubted whether dogs of this breed were very common. The skeletal evidence mainly points to a smaller type, more like a whippet. A second breed, portrayed in Middle and New Kingdom tomb scenes, displays a shorter muzzle, drooping ears and a long, hanging, or sometimes cocked, tail (cover illustration). It is usually termed a 'slughi' and resembles the modern saluki from Somalia. However, apart from these two, many indistinct types appear, resembling, for example, mastiffs or dachshunds.

Not all breeding was intentional as most dogs seem to have been pariah or street dogs, living around the houses yet not attached to a master. That these were fierce curs is evident from the New Kingdom *Tale of the Two Brothers*, in which the elder brother, returning to his spouse, who has deceived him in the manner of Potiphar's wife, is stated to have 'killed his wife and cast her to the dogs'. Another contemporary composition records the hardships of an official posted abroad. When he opened a jar of good beer, 'two hundred large dogs as well as three hundred jackals, five hundred in all, stand in readiness every day at the door of the house as often as I go out, through their smelling of the liquor'. Fortunately, he kept a little watch dog in his dwelling which rescued him repeatedly. The picture is certainly exaggerated; nevertheless it does reveal that dogs were sometimes feared.

3. A pet hound, named 'The Brave One', wearing a dog collar as he sits beneath his owner's chair. From the Theban tomb of User (TT 21), Eighteenth Dynasty. (After Davies, *Five Theban Tombs*, 1913, plates XXV and XXVIII.)

4. Pink, green and white leather dog collar with metal studs, decorated with prancing horses. From the tomb of Maiherperi, Valley of the Kings, West Thebes, Eighteenth Dynasty. (CG 24076. Courtesy of the Egyptian Museum, Cairo.)

The dog was also despised because of its cringing, servile character. Conquered enemies parading before the Pharaoh are stated, by the Egyptian scribes, to assert: 'We are indeed your dogs.' A similar sentiment is expressed by an artisan living in the desert village of the Theban necropolis workmen at Deir el-Medina. Having erred, he confesses that the god Ptah 'caused me to be as the street dogs, I being in his hand'.

Conversely, numerous tomb scenes and stelae (upright slabs) depict both pets and hunting dogs in close proximity to their masters and mistresses, sitting patiently under their chairs (figure 3) and accompanying the owner at the hunt. As a New Kingdom scribal instruction states, 'the dog obeys the word and walks behind its master'. However, it is conspicuous that dogs are never shown being fondled or played with by children, perhaps because of a fear of bites and rabies. The pet dog is the symbol of a faithful retainer. A Middle Kingdom official describes himself as 'a dog who sleeps in the tent, a hound of the bed, whom his mistress loves'. Pets wore leather collars, some multicoloured and adorned with metal studs and animal motif decoration (figure 4). A second example from the same tomb bears the dog's name: 'She of the City' (Thebes). Hounds were kept on a leash attached to the collar by a metal ring until they were loosened to pursue wild prey (figure 5).

It is not surprising, then, that dogs acquired individual names, slightly under eighty having been recorded. These refer to colour ('Blacky', 'Ebony'), to character ('Good Herdsman', 'Reliable', 'Brave One' [figure 3]), and to qualities such as speed ('Northwind', 'Antelope'). Some were even given numbers as names ('the Fifth', 'the Sixth'), on a par with the Roman first names Quintus and Sextus, possibly denoting their position in the litter. Whether the appellation 'Useless' is an insult or a name of affection remains uncertain.

On various stelae the dog names mentioned appear to be foreign, mostly Libyan, but some perhaps Nubian. A famous example, belonging to the Eleventh Dynasty Pharaoh Intef II, shows the foreign names accompanied by their Egyptian equivalents, as if the pack was called by either alternative. That dogs were imported as part of Libyan and Nubian tribute is attested by

5. Desert hunting scene with the tomb owner, his 'caddie' and a pack of hounds. From the tomb of Senbi at Meir, Twelfth Dynasty. (After Blackman, *Meir*, I, 1914, plate VI.)

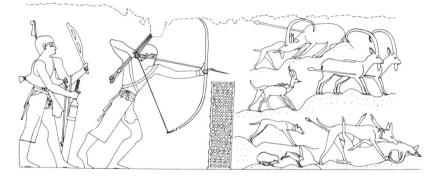

textual evidence.

Dogs also served as watch and police dogs (figure 6). A Middle Kingdom stela belonging to a member of the desert police named Kay, testifies that he patrolled the Western Desert in search of fugitives. He was subsequently promoted for his loyal service, in which he was ably assisted by the five amiable dogs depicted on the stela, two standing beside him, three lying in a register beneath. Each member of the pack has a name inscribed alongside and they were evidently faithful helpmates.

Since they loved their dogs so much, masters were wont to bury their erstwhile pets, sometimes laying them on mats in their own tombs or taking them into their sarcophagi. Dogs were even provided with individual coffins: one for a bitch, 'the beloved of her mistress', bears its own inscription. Exceptional is an Old Kingdom stela concerning a royal guard dog: 'the greyhound which kept watch over His Majesty, *Abutiu* [perhaps "With

6. Painted limestone stela of a Nubian mercenary with his wife and son. Opposite are two servants and two police dogs, one reddish brown and the other now colourless. From el-Rizeiqat, First Intermediate Period. (MFA 03.1848. Courtesy of the Museum of Fine Arts, Boston.)

7. Small limestone stela erected upon the grave of a dog called 'Lord'. From Abydos, First Dynasty. (After Quibell, *Archaic Objects*, I, 1905, page 292; now Cairo CG 14608.)

Pointed Ears"] by name', was ordered by Pharaoh to be buried and 'a sarcophagus was to be given to him from the Treasury, and very much fine cloth, incense and scented oil. His Majesty had a tomb constructed by the crews of tomb builders. He did this for him [the dog] that he might become "a Blessed".' Such a special interment may have been an exception, although the Greek historian Herodotus in his *Histories* mentions the habit of burying dogs in tombs in his day (contemporary with the Twenty-sixth Dynasty). However, a stela erected over the skeleton was not uncommon and even occurred fairly frequently during the First Dynasty at Abydos (figure 7), where the king was accompanied to the netherworld by the entire royal retinue.

This evidence substantiates the esteemed position of dogs, man's faithful and earliest companions, throughout Egyptian history.

3
Cats

In contrast with representations of the dog, which always portray the living animal, those of the cat frequently convey a religious or symbolic meaning. Stelae depicting cats actually refer to the sun god or to a female deity. In the arch of a stela in the Ashmolean Museum, Oxford, there are two felines, designated 'the Great Lady Cat' and 'the beautiful Lady Cat', and it is inscribed with a hymn to Re, 'the Great Tomcat'. Another stela, likewise from Deir el-Medina, bears the usual offering formula for 'the beautiful and gracious cat'. Exactly which goddess is described remains uncertain since several, such as Bastet, Sekhmet, Mut or Neith, were connected with felines. Bastet in particular was so frequently represented in this guise that most of the famous Late and Graeco-Roman Period cat bronzes in museum collections do not indicate the animal itself.

Moreover, depictions of cats below the chairs of their mistresses (they seem never to sit under the seat of a man) possess an additional erotic implication, their presence pointing to female sexuality (figure 8). Several such scenes are entitled 'making a feast day' and others picture banquets with nude dancing girls. A famous painting from the Theban tomb of Anen (TT 120), the Second Priest of Amun and brother of Amenophis III's wife Tiye, shows a striped cat embracing a goose with its forepaw whilst a monkey leaps in ecstasy over them. The purpose of this unnatural combination is to assert that worldly chaos is curbed and transformed into an idyllic peace. Perhaps there is also a political implication, with the cat representing the queen, and the goose Amen-Re. The embrace is then reminiscent of the ritual scenes in the Luxor Temple where Amenophis III is shown as the divine issue of a union between the god and the queen-mother.

This does not signify, however, that the animal under the chair is not also an actual pet. Symbol and reality coincide, as confirmed, for instance, by a scene in the tomb of Ipuy at Deir el-Medina (TT 217) where the cat proudly wears a silver earring, whilst her kitten is on its master's lap playing with his flapping sleeves. The figure of a young servant cradling a kitten in her arm likewise reflects real life (figure 9).

A further, very exclusive manner of portraying cats in some tomb paintings is to show them sitting in or beside the semi-circular window above the front door of the house. They are

8. A tom-cat, tied by a collar and lead to his mistress's chair leg, looks back longingly at a bowl of cat food. From the Theban tomb of May (TT 130), Eighteenth Dynasty. (After Davies, *Ancient Egyptian Paintings*, I, 1936, plate XXVII.)

sunning themselves in one of the warmest spots, yet are sheltered from the glaring sunlight. Later on this scene from daily life was no longer understood and the cat became an emblematic sphinx.

Cats comprised part of the original Egyptian fauna and those occurring in art were descendants of the African wild cat, *Felis libyca* although some interbreeding with the swamp cat is not impossible. Like their wild ancestors, the Egyptian cats were mostly lithely built tabbies, with a patchy grey coat and black, tawny or light-coloured spots and stripes. Intentional breeding was not practised, so modern breeds, such as the Persian or Manx, did not occur. The *Mau* of modern Egypt, descending from the ancient Egyptian cat, is now, however, a recognised championship breed.

The cat was first represented during the Middle Kingdom,

9. (Left) Painted wooden mirror handle in the form of a girl holding a kitten. From Abusir el-Meleq, Eighteenth Dynasty. (Ägyptisches Museum 16400. Courtesy of the Staatliche Museen zu Berlin, German Democratic Republic.)

10. (Right) Limestone sarcophagus for the beloved Lady Cat belonging to the crown prince Tuthmosis, son of Amenophis III. From Memphis, Eighteenth Dynasty. (CG 5003. Courtesy of the Egyptian Museum, Cairo.)

although 'Pussy-cat' as a female name is attested prior to this date. Moreover, cat skeletons are known from Predynastic cemeteries, indicating that they were already tamed, fed and kept, particularly as hunters of vermin in the granaries. The earliest proof for their full domestication is the Eleventh Dynasty stela in the Petrie Museum at University College London, showing a fat tom crouched under the chair of his owners and, as has been suggested, defecating behind the feet of his mistress. It is more likely to be the clumsy artistic style of the period which creates this impression.

During the Middle and New Kingdoms cats appear in fowling scenes, either in the boat or within the thicket (figure 36). Old Kingdom examples depict ichneumons or genets rather than tame cats. These representations, too, carry an emblematic implication, although some reality is not excluded. They demonstrate how the tomb owner holds sway over wildlife, in the presence of his family. The role of the cat appears to have been to flush out the roosting birds, its penetrating scent causing them to flutter and thus provide an easy prey for the fowler's throwstick. Cats were never trained to retrieve the stunned birds, since this goes against their nature. They belong essentially to the world of the farmer, as opposed to the dog, the hunter's companion.

Pets were sometimes carefully buried. At Abydos a small denuded Twelfth Dynasty pyramidal tomb contained a cruciform chamber housing seventeen cat skeletons. The excavator, Flinders Petrie, postulated that a row of rough little pots in small recesses once contained milk, this representing a rare example of a funerary offering to an animal. More elaborate is the sarcophagus which Prince Tuthmosis, an elder brother of Akhenaten, had fashioned for his beloved pet (figure 10). The offering formula describes her, placing her on a par with men, as 'Osiris, the Lady Cat', whilst she is depicted sitting before an offering table and her shabti as a mummy with a feline head.

Only one cat's name is known, 'The Pleasant One' or, more familiarly, 'Sweety'. Usually they are simply called *miu*, obviously the onomatopoeic 'mewer'. The nightly caterwauling of the tom-cat on heat is, not surprisingly, alluded to in literature. One, unfortunately rather ambiguous, text states: 'To cause to flourish him who serves God is like the wailing of a cat.' This possibly means that to cultivate the welfare of god's servants is, or should be, as natural to man as mewing is to a cat. Another composition describes the life of a dwarf. At home, with his goods and chattels adapted to his size, he can be happy, whereas in the street he suffers derision from his fellow men. The author disapproves of this reaction to his unfortunate stature, which is described as 'smaller than a tom-cat, but larger than a monkey'. Although this connection of monkeys with midgets is not unknown (figure 15), and dwarfs were employed as guardians of pets in prosperous households, this does not fully explain the comparisons.

Cats were also kept for the protection of stores against mice (figure 11), rats and smakes. A papyrus with medical spells contains the prescription: 'for not letting mice come at things: the fat of a tom, put on everything.' Whether cats were indeed killed for this purpose is doubtful. Herodotus relates how, in his time (Twenty-sixth Dynasty), when a house caught fire, people cared only for the cats, not for their property. On the death of a cat, owners were accustomed to shave their eyebrows and to transport their former pet to Bubastis, the city of the cat goddess Bastet, for burial. Clearly this is connected with the significant position of the feline deity, as are also the numerous contemporary cat mummies. In earlier periods the role of the cat was certainly less prominent.

Another feline was also tamed in ancient Egypt, albeit on a far more restricted scale. New Kingdom Pharaohs, particularly Ramesses II and III, are frequently shown in the company of a docile lion. The animal is portrayed lying beside the throne, running beside the royal horses (figure 12), or even jumping alongside the vehicle. As with representations of domestic cats, some of these scenes bear a symbolic significance.

The lion is often carved in relief on the arms of the throne as a royal emblem. Sculptures which depict a lion biting off the head of a kneeling enemy are not necessarily realistic. A statue of Ramesses VI, showing the king clasping a Libyan captive by his hair whilst a small lion strides in between the victor and the vanquished, seems metaphorically to emphasise the strength and valour of the ruler.

11. Limestone figured ostracon showing a cat with a mouse clenched between its teeth. From Deir el-Medina, West Thebes, New Kingdom. (After Vandier d'Abbadie's facsimile; now O. IFAO 2201.)

12. Ramesses II, accompanied by his panting pet lion, returning with Nubian captives. From the Great Temple at Abu Simbel, Nineteenth Dynasty. (After Wreszinski, *Atlas*, II, 1923-38, plate 181.)

However, we possess concrete evidence that Ramesses II maintained at least one tame lion in his retinue. In representations of the military camp during the Syrian Campaign, it is shown in the vicinity of horses and draught oxen, well guarded by its keeper. Perhaps this was one of the few tractable big cats, although, as early as the beginning of the First Dynasty, seven captive lion cubs were purposely placed around Horus Aha's royal tomb at Abydos. Moreover, a Middle Kingdom popular narrative describes how a magician caused a lion to follow him with its leash trailing on the ground, whilst a New Kingdom satirical composition states: 'The savage lion abandons its wrath and comes to resemble the timid donkey.'

Despite the difficulties of distinguishing symbol from reality in the depictions, and of interpreting the limited textual evidence, a picture does emerge of the cat and the lion as precious and serviceable creatures to the ancient Egyptians.

4
Monkeys

From Predynastic times onwards, monkeys formed part of Egyptian everyday life, although it is conspicuous that there are very few Middle Kingdom depictions, the dog at that time clearly being preferred. Two species mainly occur: green monkeys or vervets and baboons (figure 13). Possibly a third, the red monkey or patas, is also represented but, as the specific meanings of some Egyptian words for monkeys are not yet certain, and the artists were not accurate in rendering their colours, there is sometimes doubt as to which particular species was meant. Moreover, hybridisation was frequent. The difference between the baboon, with its mane or cape, its well developed callosities and its heavier body, and the vervet, smaller, more slender, and without cape, is clear. The latter exhibits a greenish coat and a black face and hands, whereas the patas is slightly taller with a reddish back. Among the baboons two families can be distinguished: the hamadryad and the olive or Anubis baboon, the latter being larger and with a less developed mane.

It is not known how long monkeys, at present only inhabiting countries further south, remained indigenous in Egypt; certainly they were extinct by the New Kingdom. However, imports via Nubia had already occurred during the Old Kingdom, as evidenced by frequent scenes with ships journeying north. They transport monkeys which are clambering all over the mast and rigging. In New Kingdom tribute representations they are borne by elephant tusk porters and cling to the necks of giraffes (figure 44). Probably many died fairly soon, for these primates are susceptible to various diseases, such as tumours, rickets and, especially, tuberculosis, all detected in embalmed specimens.

It is unclear why monkeys were imported, but for baboons there may have been a religious motive. At dawn and dusk, after leaving or before moving into their lairs, colonies congregate to chatter loudly. This was interpreted as greeting the sun; consequently baboons became connected with the solar cult. Their sculptured forms with raised hands frequently adorn the pedestals of obelisks. The economic advantage of keeping monkeys, however, was minimal. They may have been adopted in daily life purely for the delight of witnessing their buffoonery. Moreover, these intelligent animals are highly adaptable to environmental conditions and contact with humans. Baboons, especially males,

13. Cosmetic objects. (Left) Bronze razor with decorative handle in the form of a long-tailed monkey wearing collar and belt and holding a bunch of dom-palm nuts. (Right) Ebony quintuple kohl tube of the scribe It, the left side depicting a squatting female baboon, named 'the Fine One', eating a dom-palm nut. Both unprovenanced, Eighteenth Dynasty. (UC. 30135; 30136).

although sweet with children and young animals, are unpredictable in their behaviour and therefore less suitable as pets, although the females were taken into the household. It is the figure of a baboon which is employed to determine the word for aggression. Its nature was already acknowledged in an Old Kingdom *Pyramid Utterance* to a thieving baboon deity: 'Get back, Babi, red of ears and purple of hindquarters. You have taken the cutlet [the meat offering] of your goddess to your mouth.'

Vervets, particularly, were adopted as pets. They sometimes wear a collar or a belt, even bracelets and anklets. Frequently depicted under the chairs of their owners (figure 14), they also

14. Limestone double relief with a long-tailed monkey tied under its owner's chair. From the tomb of Merymery at Saqqara, Nineteenth Dynasty. (AP 6. Courtesy of the Rijksmuseum van Oudheden, Leiden.)

appear at their mistresses' toilette, as cosmetic objects (figure 13), and even in erotic scenes. As with cats, these monkeys often convey female sexuality, which is not surprising in view of their conspicuous behaviour. Regarded as lascivious because of their habit of standing on their hind legs and exhibiting their brightly coloured genitalia, they were both admired and feared for their sexual potency.

On a par with other pets, monkeys were sometimes given special interments. A mummified example, possibly belonging to Amenophis II, was found in a shaft in the Valley of the Kings, together with a dog. Notorious is the case of Maatkare, a Twenty-first Dynasty princess, who occupied the supreme religious office of 'God's Wife of Amun'. Such women were supposed to be virgins but in her coffin a small mummy was discovered nestling against her own mortal remains. Whole stories, even a novel, have been woven around what seemed to imply an illicit relationship, until recent X-rays revealed that the alleged baby was her pet female baboon.

There are many representations of baboons and green monkeys accompanying dogs, all held on leashes by keepers. During the Old Kingdom these guardians were dwarfs, in the New Kingdom mostly Nubians. The connection with dwarfs who acted as dancers and jesters, implies a similar role for the monkeys (figure 15). In the New Kingdom these midgets were, at least in theory, regarded as normal human beings but monkeys were still used for dancing and foolery. An instruction by a father for his son states that 'The monkey carries the stick [for dancing], though its mother did not carry it', meaning that the clever animal was capable of learning tricks. So they are upheld before pupils as examples of teachability: 'Monkeys are taught to dance', or even 'the monkey understands words'. It was this innate intelligence that induced the Egyptians to connect Thoth, the god of writing and wisdom, with the baboon.

Not all scenes with monkeys reflect reality, certainly not drawings on *ostraca* (broken pottery sherds or limestone flakes). That the animals could be taught to play various musical instruments (figure 50) is inconceivable, nor does it appear plausible that they could carry yokes for watering the garden. Another joke is the figured ostracon showing a monkey scratching a girl's nose (figure 16). The animal was added afterwards, in

15. A dwarf, named Mereri, playing with a monkey on a lead. From the mastaba of Nefer, called Idu, at Giza, Sixth Dynasty. (After Junker, *Giza*, VIII, 1947, figure 35; now Hildesheim PM 2390.)

16. Painted potsherd with a monkey scratching a girl's prominent nose. From the Ramesseum, West Thebes, New Kingdom. (UC 15946.)

17. (Below) Men picking and packing figs, whilst monkeys help themselves to fruit in the tree. From the tomb of Khnumhotep at Beni Hasan, Twelfth Dynasty. (After Davies, *Ancient Egyptian Paintings*, I, 1936, plate VII.)

a clumsier style, to what was a trial piece for a tomb painting. Perhaps this was the jest of a fellow student, for the sketch derives from an art school. A similar intention may be suggested for an Old Kingdom tomb scene of the launching of a boat. A shipwright is crawling under the hulk to remove a brake-block, and another pours water on the ground to facilitate the gliding, whilst the foreman stands nearby supervising the manoeuvre. At the stern of the vessel a baboon, wielding a stick, gesticulates as if he himself directs the operation. Was this an incident really witnessed by the draughtsman? In view of the monkey's power of imitation, this seems not improbable. Whatever the situation, it struck the ancient artist as comic.

Scenes in which monkeys climb trees and pick fruit (figure 17), or sit and attempt to pilfer dom-palm nuts from network sacks are certainly realistic. Dom-palm nuts constitute the basic diet of baboons (figure 13), together with figs, grapes and other fruit. That the animals are helping the workers at the harvest is unlikely.

Perhaps the only real utility of monkeys was their function as assistants to the police, depicted in some Old Kingdom tombs (figure 18). The officers often carry truncheons terminating in hands. Some dwarf guardians bear similar cudgels for chastising their charges. In the reform decree of Pharaoh Horemheb, 'keepers of monkeys' are cited as one of the classes of officials who abused their power during the unruly years of Akhenaten. Possibly they were corrupt policemen who had counterfeited the grain measure and extracted bakshishes in the form of linen, vegetables and fruit.

In a few instances the names of individual monkeys have been transmitted but far fewer than names of dogs. Those of baboons are unbelievably complex, such as 'His-father-awaits-him' or even the sentence 'When the foreign country is pacified the land

18. Police baboons arrest a thief in the market place. The text above reads: 'Fear for this baboon.' From the mastaba of Tepemankh at Saqqara, Fifth Dynasty. (After Stevenson Smith, *History of Egyptian Sculpture and Painting*, 1946, figure 225c; now Cairo CG 1556.)

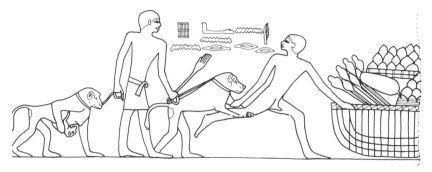

is happy', reminiscent of horse nomenclature. One case of a simple name is fairly certain. Under the seat of a woman on a stela in the Leiden museum 'Dearie' is written, although the sculptor forgot to carve a figure. Another stela of the same lady, now in Rio de Janeiro, shows, below the chair, a monkey eating fruit from a hamper but does not carry the animal's name. Very probably the same animal is meant.

Although the usefulness of the monkey, which played a significant part in Egyptian life and religion, may be small, it was as favourite a companion as a dog or a cat. Monkeys were popular because of their clownish antics and capacity for imitation, which clearly amused onlookers.

19. Wooden model of a cattle stable. From the tomb of Meket-Re at Deir el-Bahri, West Thebes, Eleventh Dynasty. (MMA 20.3.9. Courtesy of the Metropolitan Museum of Art, Rogers Fund and Edward S. Harkness Gift, 1920.)

5
Livestock

In his tomb, Renni, the late Seventeenth Dynasty mayor of El Kab, relates how he inspected his livestock comprising 122 head of cattle, 100 sheep, 1200 goats and 1500 pigs. Such an inventory seems fairly indicative of the composition of the herds on a nobleman's estate.

Farmstead cattle, descended from aurochs, were perhaps domesticated in Egypt in prehistoric times. Wild cattle, as amplified by numerous texts and representations, still occurred and were hunted during the New Kingdom. Apart from the humped zebu, introduced from Syria as a draught animal during the Eighteenth Dynasty and regarded as foreign, two types of oxen, longhorn and shorthorn, were distinguished. The latter entered the country later, perhaps during the Old Kingdom, and gradually supplanted the former. Both types were occasionally polled. Egyptian terminology differentiates age (calf, heifer, yearling), sex (bull, cow, bullock) and colour (black, red, white, dappled, piebald, brindled and so on).

The main distinction was between oxen confined to stables for fattening and slaughter (figure 19) and the herds roaming freely in the pastures, mainly used as draught animals for the plough (figure 20), for threshing and for their milk (figure 1). Adult Egyptians, in contrast with other ancient peoples, were evidently capable of digesting milk without experiencing lactose malabsorption. Ageing pasture cattle were slaughtered for food.

A type of transhumance was practised whereby in winter the herds stayed in the Nile valley, moving in the hot summers to the cool waters of the Delta marshlands. Cowherds watched the beasts but, in order to prevent theft, pasture oxen were branded, mostly on their foreheads or haunches, with the marks of their owners (figure 21). For this purpose, the state or a temple, but also rich individuals, used bronze cattle brands (figure 22). A young man in a love poem likewise desires that his beloved may 'brand him with her seal'.

Beef provided food for the prosperous, although a slaughtered ox, providing portions for a thousand or more people, could hardly be consumed immediately. The meat was therefore mostly salted and dried, as indicated by inscriptions on the vessels in which it was transported. Beef formed the prime offering to the gods, other meat, apart from venison and fowl, being too lowly esteemed. Cattle hide provided leather to make, for example, thongs, sandals, shields, chair seats and webbing. Horn and bone were also useful by-products. Because of the lack of trees and bushes in the Nile valley, the dung of cattle, like that from other animals, was essential for fuel.

Although cattle were bred in Egypt (figure 23), they were also imported in substantial numbers from neighbouring countries as booty, tribute and merchandise. Cattle represented high social status and economic value and owners were proud to display their stock, so much so that their frequent occurrence on tomb walls may convey a distorted picture. Nevertheless, one moderately wealthy farmer possessed, according to his account papyri, three bulls, eleven cows, six young animals (one bull) and fifteen

20. Wooden tomb model of a peasant ploughing with a pair of yoked piebald oxen, unprovenanced, Middle Kingdom. (EA 52947. Courtesy of the Trustees of the British Museum.)

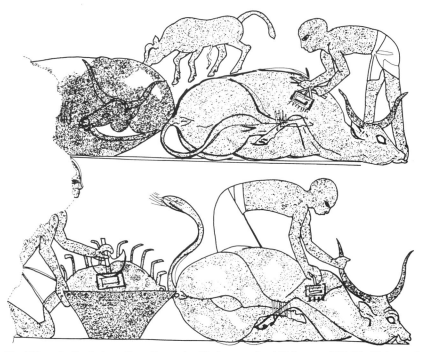

21. (Above) Cattle branding. From the Theban tomb of Nebamun (TT 90), Eighteenth Dynasty. (After Davies, *The Tombs of Two Officials of Tuthmosis IV*, 1923, plate XXXII.)

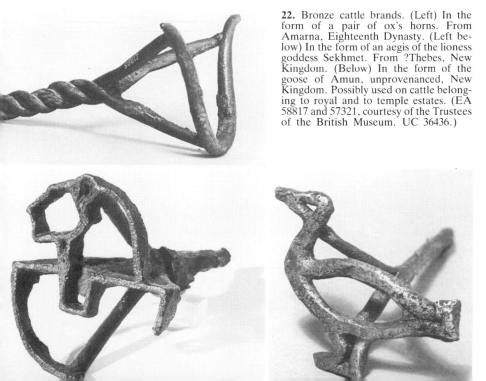

22. Bronze cattle brands. (Left) In the form of a pair of ox's horns. From Amarna, Eighteenth Dynasty. (Left below) In the form of an aegis of the lioness goddess Sekhmet. From ?Thebes, New Kingdom. (Below) In the form of the goose of Amun, unprovenanced, New Kingdom. Possibly used on cattle belonging to royal and to temple estates. (EA 58817 and 57321, courtesy of the Trustees of the British Museum. UC 36436.)

draught oxen. Even a more well-to-do artisan at Deir el-Medina could own one or two oxen. Temples acquired substantial herds: Ramesses III presented his Theban mortuary temple at Medinet Habu with 1309 head of cattle, of various ages and both sexes, from captured Libyan booty.

From the Early Dynastic Period onwards the cattle tax constituted a significant source of state revenue. That officials, in troubled times, abused their power to collect it is evident from the decree of Horemheb which describes troops going from house to house to requisition every available hide. A piece of pessimistic literature from the disorderly First Intermediate Period relates: 'See, cattle stray with none to bring them back; everyone fetches for himself and brands with his name. He who could not find plough oxen [now] owns cattle.' This confirms that poor farmers did not own draught animals and were forced to hire them.

Calves cost about as much as donkeys, a cow twice and a bull four or five times as much, each individual value depending upon the quality of the beast. The price for beef is unknown as it was seldom sold, although there is evidence that the temples reverted part of the offerings. The god received only the head and a leg, the remainder going for human consumption.

Cows received individual names of various types, such as 'Fine Inundation', 'The Pigeon' and 'Good Counsel'. Herds bore compounds of a royal name plus an epithet: 'Ramesses-Conqueror-of-the-Meswesh [Libyans] -at-the-Water-of-the Sun'.

23. A cowherd delivering a panting cow of her calf, while his overseer makes a magical good luck gesture. From Saqqara, Fifth Dynasty. (After Wild, *Le tombeau de Ti*, II, 1953, plate CXXIV.)

24. Household articles. (Above) Wooden dish adorned with four projecting rams' heads. From Kahun, Late Middle Kingdom. (UC 16680.) (Below) Bronze razor, the blade decorated with a solid copper goat, unprovenanced, New Kingdom. (EA 26262. Courtesy of the Trustees of the British Museum.)

Scribal compositions present the tamed ox as an almost human example to pupils: 'The cow will plough on the return of the year; it begins to listen to the cowherd, it can all but speak.'

Sheep and goats are infrequently depicted on household objects (figure 24). The Egyptians referred to them by a single term, 'small cattle', thereby ignoring their considerable differences. Goats, being more intelligent, can better adapt themselves to a harsh environment: in Egypt, to the aridity of the desert. They have a greater resistance to epidemics and are also more fertile than sheep. Most important, goats feed themselves by browsing (figure 25), whereas sheep demand grass. Accordingly,

25. Goats browsing and eating leaves helped by a goatherd who tears down the foliage using a hooked stick. From Saqqara, Fifth Dynasty. (After Moussa and Altenmüller, *The Tomb of Nefer and Ka-Hay*, 1971, plate 18.)

goats far outnumbered sheep, as attested by both excavations and textual evidence. For instance, goats were common at Deir el-Medina, yet no sheep are recorded.

Egypt possessed in succession two different races of sheep, which are only once depicted together (figure 26). Until the Middle Kingdom there was a hairy thin-tailed breed, with corkscrew-shaped horns extending laterally from the head. It already showed an improvement on its wild ancestor in that the kemp was more woolly and the hair grew all the year round,

26. Shepherds leading a flock of sheep comprising both the hairy and woolly breeds. From the tomb of Khnumhotep at Beni Hasan, Twelfth Dynasty. (After Newberry, *Beni Hasan*, I, 1893, plate XXX.)

whereas the earlier sheep would moult in spring, discarding hair all over the grazing area. The hairy sheep was kept mainly for its meat, milk and skin, and the flocks were used for treading seed into the fields after sowing. Woollen textiles are accordingly scarce until the Middle Kingdom.

The later breed, with its shorter and fatter tail, bore recurving horns such as distinguish the ram-headed forms of the god Amen-Re from all other ram deities, such as Khnum, which exhibit the Old Kingdom type. As the wool of this new race was well suited to spinning and weaving, woollen fabrics are not rare in later periods.

Shears do not occur before the Third Intermediate Period, so wool was evidently plucked or cut with a knife. In contrast to many ancient cultures, shearing was never combined with religious festivities, reflecting both the negligible economic role of sheep and also the late introduction of the woolly breed.

Although a selective goat-breeding policy was unknown, goats were kept for their meat, skin and perhaps milk, though less importantly for their hair. Goat's meat, like pork, constituted party fare for peasants and was never used in offerings. Goatskin served for diverse leather objects, particularly water sacks (see the 'caddie' in figure 5), whilst goat hair was processed at the workmen's village east of Akhenaten's capital at Amarna.

Prices of sheep are unrecorded but many for goats have been preserved. Their value was less than that of a pig and approximately one-tenth of that of a donkey or a calf.

According to Herodotus, the pig was regarded as unclean in ancient Egypt: 'If a man in passing accidentally touches a pig, he hurries to the river and plunges in with all his clothes on.' Moreover, no man would give his daughter in marriage to a swineherd.

At first glance, the evidence tends to corroborate Herodotus' statement, for pigs are never depicted on temple walls and feature in only a handful of tombs, mainly of the early Eighteenth Dynasty, and on a unique and delightful Old Kingdom relief (figure 27). Pig bones have never been found in a tomb, nor does pork feature amongst the temple offerings.

Nevertheless, the pig was already domesticated in the Neolithic Period, doubtless from the wild boar which, until modern times, frequently roamed the Delta and Fayumic marshlands. The older word for pig was synonymous with that for both the wild boar and for the hippopotamus. Only later was a specific term coined for the household pig. Characteristically high-legged, with a very

27. A swineherd weans a suckling piglet using milk placed on his tongue from the jar held by his colleague. From the mastaba of Kagemni at Saqqara, Sixth Dynasty. (After Firth and Gunn, *Teti Pyramid Cemeteries*, II, 1926, plate 52.)

slender snout and a dark and bristly skin, the same type still inhabits the Coptic towns and villages of modern Egypt.

Although New Kingdom scenes depict pigs treading seed into the soil, partly replacing the hairy sheep, they were principally kept for their meat. A stela of Amenhotep, the chief steward of Amenophis III, testifies that he donated not only fields and slaves to a Memphite statue of his royal master but also one thousand pigs and one thousand other animals, probably piglets. So, surprisingly swine were attached to religious institutions, providing food for the lower temple personnel.

Moreover, modern excavations at settlement sites, notably Memphis, Amarna, Tell Dab'a and Elephantine, amply demonstrate extensive pig farming. Indeed, in every ancient town the number of pig bones, in relation to those of other animals, is impressive. Specialised farrowing units, 2 metres (6 feet 6 inches) square, have been uncovered in the workmen's village at Amarna. Within each pen, a small walled sty confined the litter, only the sow being able to pass its high threshold into the larger feeding yard.

Even in a desert village pigs were easy to maintain on household scraps, although they also received grain. Pork was poor man's food, beef representing the prerogative of the rich. Pigs cost two or three times as much as a goat, and one-sixth as much as a donkey.

A satirical treatise compares the potter, who 'grubs in the

mud', with the dirty pig. However, unlike in modern languages, the word for pig was not used as an insult.

On his Abydos stela the Twelfth Dynasty steward Mentuweser enumerates his functions, describing himself as overseer of three thousand peasants, of cattle, goats, donkeys, sheep and swine. The order roughly reflects the ancient Egyptians' appreciation of these animals, horses at that period still being unknown. As a comparison, records from Saxon England provide a scale of values: horse, 120 pence; ox, 30 pence; cow, 20 pence; pig, 10 pence; and sheep, 5 pence.

6
Donkeys and horses

Donkeys played an essential role in Pharaonic Egypt, as they still do in the Nile valley, as the principal load-carriers. Domesticated horses, introduced only just before the New Kingdom, were chiefly used for warfare and by their relative rarity bestowed prestige upon their wealthy owners. The camel, although known from prehistoric times (as was the donkey), was not employed in daily life before the Graeco-Roman Period.

The Egyptian word for donkey was *eeyore*, clearly a form of onomatopoeia. The same word frequently occurs with the connotation 'ass-load', a vague measure of quantity for bulky and relatively cheap goods, thus reflecting the primary function of the donkey as a beast of burden. A saddle-pack, comprising a basket or leathern sack fastened on to the back by means of ropes and straps, enabled the donkey to carry weights of up to 50 kg (100 pounds) divided into equal loads on each side. A saddle-cloth, consisting of a piece of fringed textile with weft-loop pile, was first laid over the animal's back to protect its skin.

Numerous tomb scenes (figure 28) portray donkeys bedecked in this fashion, mainly being used for the transport of sheaves from the fields to the threshing floors and of grain to the granaries. Like oxen, they were employed for threshing itself, a job for which their sharp hoofs made them particularly suitable. Their use as draught animals is less well substantiated but it seems that plough donkeys existed, and two New Kingdom texts refer to asses pulling a chariot. Three Old Kingdom reliefs portray the owner being transported to the fields in an elaborate palanquin suspended over the backs of two donkeys (figure 29). Although only foreigners are shown riding on donkeys, it cannot be supposed that ordinary Egyptians did not travel in a similar fashion. Rather, these tomb representations, with their religious preoccupation, do not fully represent the minutiae of daily life.

Systematic donkey breeding was undertaken; foals frequently appear in delightful depictions (figure 30) and in written contracts. Mules were rare in ancient Egypt as stallions were too valuable to be used just for breeding and because of the likelihood of producing undesirable hybrid offspring. Additionally, such foals are generally sterile. The donkey was easy to maintain, demanding scant attention and being able to survive on very little water and poor-quality forage, browsing, when allowed

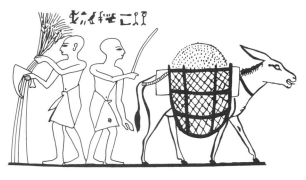

28. Donkeys at the harvest. (Upper left) A she-ass in front of a granary. From the Theban tomb of Ahmose (TT 241), Eighteenth Dynasty. (After Shorter, in *Journal of Egyptian Archaeology*, XVI (1930), plate XV.) (Upper right) 'Suty loads the donkeys.' From Thebes (TT 16), Nineteenth Dynasty. (After Baud-Drioton, *Le tombeau de Panehsy*, 1932, figure 22. (Right) Donkeys on the threshing floor. From Saqqara, Fifth Dynasty. (After van de Walle, *La chapelle funéraire de Neferirtenef*, 1978, plate 12; now Brussels E 2465).

to, on desert scrubs. Nearer the floodplain, controlled herding occurred, and fodder was probably supplied if the asses were placed in pens overnight.

The animal could work up to its fortieth year or even longer. A text from Deir el-Medina relates how an ass died from being 'hot', probably from a high fever. Another fell ill from being beaten and having to carry too many people. Possessors are recorded as having taken care of their sick donkeys. A noteworthy comment, 'I have seen a good donkey, even the best. You must accept it. Really, its face is something great', displays an unexpected appreciation for the appearance of the beast. However, a buyer would refuse a particular ass because it was 'bad', meaning feeble, underfed, or such like, rather than that it was no beauty! The attitude to the animal is expressed in the proverb: 'When there is work to do, get a donkey, when there is

29. Donkeys for transport: (above) Niankhkhnum is borne to the fields in a palanquin suspended between two asses; (right) a donkey loaded with young gazelles from the desert. From Saqqara, Fifth Dynasty. (After Moussa and Altenmüller, *Das Grab des Nianchchnum und Chnumhotep*, 1977, plate 42 and figure 13.)

fodder, fetch an ox.'

The purchase price of an average donkey was fairly high, equalling the price of a cow or a coffin. No distinction was drawn between male and female asses, so variations in value simply reflect quality and the age of the beasts. Owning a donkey was beyond the means of the mass of the peasants, who were supplied with donkeys by the landowners, primarily during spring, the season of the harvest.

The horse was adopted from the Hyksos, the Asiatic conquerors of Egypt, at the end of the Second Intermediate Period. Always a prestige animal, it was kept exclusively by the upper classes for war, hunting and short-distance transport (figure 31).

30. The stock-taking of asses. From the tomb of Baqt at Beni Hasan, Twelfth Dynasty. (After Champollion, *Monuments*, 1845, plate CCCXCI.)

Several words connected with horses were borrowed directly from the Semitic languages spoken by the Hyksos, although for most there existed pure Egyptian equivalents. Possibly these foreign terms were mainly in vogue amongst the wealthy owners, while the old Egyptian words represented common vernacular.

Ancient horses were fairly small: using the yoke measurements of surviving chariots, an average height of 1.35 metres (4 feet 6 inches) has been calculated. However, the oldest horse skeleton, excavated at Buhen in Nubia, and possibly dating from the Middle Kingdom, is about 1.50 metres (4 feet 11 inches) high. The horse bones found carefully buried in front of the Theban tomb of Senenmut (TT 71), the favourite of Queen Hatshepsut,

31. Wall-painting showing horses harnessed to chariots. Upper register: lively chestnut and greyish-black horses. Lower register: docile greyish-blue ?Przewalski's horses. From the Theban tomb of Nebamun (TT 146), Eighteenth Dynasty. (EA 37982. Courtesy of the Trustees of the British Museum.)

are also slightly larger than average. Although horse breeding was not unknown in Egypt, a large proportion were imported, either by trade or as spoils of war, from Syria or further north. The Karnak *Annals,* listing booty captured by Tuthmosis III at Megiddo, specify: 2041 horses, 191 young animals, both male and female, six stallions, and a number of foals.

Systematic breeding produced elegant and swift animals with long bodies and slender legs; speed, not power, clearly being the main objective. A light two-wheeled chariot, requiring minimal muscular effort, was invariably pulled by a pair (team) of horses (figure 31). The unique team lower in the same painting possibly represents Przewalski's horses rather than mules. Bareback riding seems to have been mainly restricted to foreigners and scouts. As only a handful of representations (figure 32) picture the Egyptians so engaged, they presumably regarded the practice as undignified. Prince Tefnakhte of Sais, in the Twenty-fifth Dynasty, is described fleeing from his conquerors: 'He mounted a horse without [even] asking [for] his chariot.' This was clearly an ignominious retreat!

Regrettably, no ancient Egyptian horse-training manuals, comparable with the Greek *Treatise on Horsemanship* by Xenophon, survive, although contemporary examples have been excavated in both the Assyrian and Hittite capitals. Once again, the Egyptians derived such techniques from the Near East, but their lack of available training space proved a hindrance. Chariot races, famous from ancient Rome, were never held. However, excavations near Malkata, on the Theban West Bank, have revealed a straight stretch of swept desert, 4 km long by 120

32. Bronze toilette implement in the form of a horse and rider, unprovenanced, Eighteenth Dynasty. (EA 36314. Courtesy of the Trustees of the British Museum.)

33. Bronze toilette implement in the form of a plumed ?royal galloping horse, unprovenanced, Eighteenth Dynasty. (UC 26935.)

metres wide (2½ miles by 138 yards), representing what may have been a training course. A hill at one side perhaps formed the grandstand, whilst a platform in the vicinity, on which tents and awnings were erected, may have functioned as a royal rest-house.

Time and skill were an essential prerequisite in such training and handling. Scribal literature, which often compares the breaking-in of horses with that of youths, portrays the horse as wiser than unruly pupils! With their newly acquired expertise and, for antiquity, amazing speed the charioteers soon felt themselves to be far superior to the common infantryman. The powerful weaponry of the chariotry likewise became the pride of the pharaohs. As its commanders they were invariably depicted in chariots for both battle and the chase.

In characteristic Egyptian fashion, such sentiments found open expression. Above the representation of the chariot and horses of Paheri, an early Eighteenth Dynasty mayor of El Kab, the controlling charioteer exhorts his beasts: 'Stand still, do not resist, you fine team of the mayor, beloved of his master, of which he boasts to everyone.' Even more illustrative is one of the stelae found between the paws of the Sphinx at Giza, which describes how Amenophis II, whilst still a young prince, 'adored horses and delighted in them. He was tenacious in working them, one who knew their nature, and was conversant with their training, having close acquaintance with their disposition.' He was accustomed to harness them with the bridle himself, and drove from Memphis to Giza in order to visit the Pyramids and Sphinx. Ramesses III is depicted in the royal stables: 'inspecting the horses which his [own] hands have trained'.

Thus the teams of horses were made up of well loved personalities, and were often, particularly in the case of royal horses, assigned individual names. The teams used by Ramesses II in his Asiatic campaigns were called: 'Victory in Thebes' and 'Mut-is-contented'. Further examples are: 'Amun gives Might', 'Repulsers of Foreigners' and 'Tramplers of Foreign Countries'.

Horses seem mostly to have been state property, royal equids usually being distinguished by plumed head-dresses (figure 33). However, the upper classes may have possessed them privately (figure 34). The state barracks excavated at Amarna were designed to house up to two hundred animals. The chariotry here played a role in the Household Brigade, both as a guard of honour and as a police flying squad. The dowager Queen Tiye also possessed stables in this city, as evidenced by a seal for stamping a clay imprint (figure 35). Indeed, apart from their breaking-in and training, horses were invariably confined to stables, where they received daily rations of grass and straw, oats being unknown in ancient Egypt. A model letter relates: 'The horse teams of my lord are well; I have their allotted measure mixed before them, and their grooms bring them the best grass

34. The chamberlain Tutu riding home, amidst cheers, after his investiture at the palace. From the tomb of Tutu at Amarna, Eighteenth Dynasty. (After Davies, *El Amarna*, VI, 1908, plate XX.)

35. Limestone seal with the hieroglyphic signs for 'rich in horses' flanking the cartouche of Queen Tiye. From Amarna, Eighteenth Dynasty. (UC 376A.)

from the marshes. I assign grass to them daily and give ointment to rub them every month, and their chiefs of the stable trot them every ten days.' The leisured lifestyle of these well esteemed animals thus contrasts sharply with that of the valued but exploited donkey.

7
Birds

Ornithologists have recognised more than seventy bird families and species in Egyptian art. Several, such as the cormorant, spoonbill, flamingo, owl and quail, occur more or less exclusively as hieroglyphs, over sixty of which portray birds or parts of them. The lapwing, conspicuous because of its long wispy crest, is mainly used to indicate 'common folk'.

Clearly the Egyptians delighted in the elegance and beauty of brightly coloured birds, as evidenced by numerous fowling scenes. That from the Theban tomb of Nebamun (TT 146) is a splendid example (figure 36). Moreover, such pictures conveyed concepts veiled from the modern eye. The tame Nile goose, poised on the bow of the skiff, uttering its strident 'kek-kek', is not so much a decoy as an erotic allusion. The presence on the wobbly papyrus raft of Nebamun's wife, attired in her best clothes, seems unrealistic, as do the fat cat and roosting birds precariously perched on fragile papyrus stalks and umbels. These elements simply strengthen the symbolism, whilst the accompanying text runs: 'Enjoying oneself by looking at the beauty in the place of eternal life.' The representation thus refers to reproduction, regeneration, and rebirth in the netherworld. It is not surprising, therefore, that several of the gaily painted fowl are difficult to identify, as both their colours and their anatomical details are misleading. Nevertheless, it is undeniable that both the artist and his contemporaries greatly admired the grace of these feathered creatures.

This is further attested by the excavated remains of the North Palace at Amarna. One of its courtyards contained a central pond around which a variety of water birds was kept, as evidenced by the famous murals in a cubicle which depict a kingfisher, a rock pigeon and a turtle dove in a landscape devoid of human life. A picture window in another cubicle enabled the onlooker to appreciate the beauty of the fluttering fowl.

The same pleasure led the Egyptians to take into captivity the golden oriole, renowned for its sweet call, the hoopoe, with its marked black-tipped crest, and the shrill-voiced lapwing. The latter two birds were popular children's pets, as was the crane, which is once even depicted sporting a collar (figure 37).

Only the greylag and the white-fronted goose were fully domesticated, breeding in confinement. However, other geese

36. Wall-painting with fowling scene. The tomb owner is aided by three decoy herons and his pet cat. From the Theban tomb of Nebamun (TT 146), Eighteenth Dynasty. (EA 37977. Courtesy of the Trustees of the British Museum.)

species, as well as ducks (especially the pintail), cranes (both the common and the demoiselle crane), pigeons (rock pigeon and turtle dove), were treated as half-domesticated animals, being represented from the Predynastic Period onwards (figure 38). The fact that 'Goose' and 'Pigeon' occur as personal names indicates that these birds were particularly popular.

Large numbers of fowl were consumed by the élite. Hence they regularly appear among the offerings to both the gods and the dead. A surviving Second Dynasty funerary repast from Saqqara consisted of pigeon stew and a cooked quail in addition to bread, porridge, fruit and kidneys, ribs and legs of beef.

One of the best known waterfowl from Pharaonic Egypt is the Nile goose, although it seldom occurs in offering scenes and texts

37. Bronze toilette implement in the form of a young common crane wearing a collar, unprovenanced, Eighteenth Dynasty. (UC 36425).

or in tangible remains, doubtless because it is a poor table bird. Moreover, since it was the sacred animal of Amun, and because it had a gluttonous nature and was aggressive towards other birds and even towards men, it was considered both useless and obnoxious. This appears evident from the eloquent simile of an idle pupil as 'worse than the Nile goose of the riverbank, busy with mischief. It spends the summer in ravaging the dates, the winter in destroying the seed grain; its free time of the year in pursuit of the peasants. One cannot catch it by snaring. One does not offer it in the temple, sharp-eyed bird that does not work!'

Birds such as the oriole, the hoopoe and the roller, which was a pest of the orchards, were snared in small spring-traps or fine-meshed nets suspended from tree-tops. Similarly despised was the perky little house sparrow, an omnivorous feeder, which lived around the settlements as it does today. Its use as a hieroglyph indicated all that was bad and evil, for, as a text states, 'The sparrow means want upon the peasant'.

Some birds are conspicuously rare in tomb scenes. The ibis, sacred to Thoth, the god of wisdom and writing, is, by inference, almost absent from representations of daily life. Yet a depiction under the master's seat proves it could be treated as a pet. The bird is used for two different hieroglyphs, the modern name being directly derived from the Egyptian. In the Late Period ibises were bred on a massive scale in sanctuaries and mummified to meet the demands of a flourishing pilgrim industry. One and a half million have been excavated from the Saqqara catacombs alone.

The saddlebill stork is present merely as a hieroglyphic sign. Perhaps its route to Central Africa in antiquity passed over the Red Sea, turning inland at the latitude of Qena, so bypassing the Memphite capital, where the canon of tomb representations was evolved. A few pictures portray the chicken (red junglefowl), one being a rooster sketched on an ostracon (figure 39). It may also feature in the Karnak *Annals* of Tuthmosis III amongst Asiatic booty as 'the bird that gives birth every day'. Yet, it remained foreign until the Persian Conquest. Eggs were only obtained from waterfowl, whose feathers were also used for cushion stuffing.

The Egyptians were familiar with such a profusion of birdlife because Egypt is on the major migratory route between Europe and Africa. The Delta is also a wintering area for fowl from northern climes. Since the large exhausted flocks nestling and

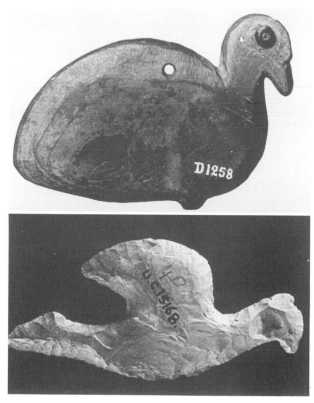

38. Graceful objects: (above) green schist duck-shaped palette, with carnelian eye; (below) flint carving of a flying pigeon. Both unprovenanced, Predynastic. (D 1258; courtesy of the Musée d'art et d'histoire, Geneva. UC 15168.)

39. Limestone figured ostracon showing a rooster. From the Valley of the Kings, West Thebes, Nineteenth Dynasty. (EA 68539. Courtesy of the Trustees of the British Museum.)

sheltering in the marshes and orchards proved easy prey for the trapper, domestication was not a prime concern. The few surviving prices for birds (?pigeons) indicate that their value was lower than that of a pair of papyrus sandals or a simple basket, and hardly higher than a small loaf of flat, round bread.

Nevertheless, from the Old Kingdom onwards some species were kept in poultry yards, in aviaries, or in cramped cages reminiscent of modern battery farms. Fairly tame species could be maintained in the open, as evidenced by a text of Tuthmosis III: 'My Majesty created a flock of greylag geese, in order to fill the aviary for the daily offerings to the god [Amen-Re]'. A decree of Seti I states that on a bird farm of Osiris at Abydos 'their number is like the sand of the shore'. Indeed, at Karnak a fowl-yard has been excavated which connects with the water in the Sacred Lake by means of a sloping underground gallery, too small for a man. A stela discovered in the vicinity relates that the enclosure contained geese, cranes, swans, pigeons and other fowl to supply the divine offering. That enormous numbers of birds were involved is substantiated by a papyrus of Ramesses III recording that, during his 31-year reign, the Pharaoh delivered over 680,000 geese to the temples.

40. Force-feeding geese, ducks and cranes in an aviary. From the mastaba of Sopduhotep at Saqqara, Fifth Dynasty. (After Wreszinski, *Atlas*, III, 1923-38, plate 83; now East Berlin 14642.)

Likewise palaces, luxurious villas, and even modest workmen's dwellings contained poultry yards and aviaries, as proved by numerous tomb scenes and excavated settlements. The pigeon castles, now so characteristic of the Egyptian landscape, are unattested in antiquity.

To a stately mansion of a high official belong 'a fowl-yard and an aviary with greylag geese, byres full of oxen, a breeding bird

41. Men plucking and roasting waterfowl. From the mastaba of Nefer-seshem-Ptah at Saqqara, Sixth Dynasty. (After Wreszinski, *Atlas*, III, 1923-38, plate 81.)

pool with geese, and horses in the stable'. Although such enclosures are frequently represented in Old Kingdom tombs, they rarely occur in New Kingdom art. However, one relief, possibly deriving from Amarna and now in Florence, shows an open-air fowl-run penetrated by the sun-rays, with geese, ducks and ibises in and around a pond. Probably a covering net prevented the birds from escaping or else their wings were clipped. Products of aviculture feature in account papyri; a Thirteenth Dynasty text from the royal household lists geese, ducks, pigeons and swans among the food delivered to various courtiers. An unpublished text from the time of Seti I, now in the British Museum, presents information on one of the palace fowl-yards which contained thousands of birds of various species.

The fowl were fed with milled grain and bread pellets, sometimes even being force-fed in order to improve their flavour (figure 40). After slaughter they were plucked and then either roasted to be eaten immediately or dried, salted and pickled in large amphorae for later consumption (figure 41).

Thus the birds of the Nile valley formed a source both of joy to the eye and food for the body. Moreover, the goose and the duck with turned-back head (figure 48) provided symbols of eroticism and rebirth.

8
Pharaoh's menagerie

Egyptian rulers took considerable pleasure in exotic fauna, which served their glorification in the chase. In addition to adorning their palaces, rare creatures were also sometimes presented to fellow potentates.

The hippopotamus and the rhinoceros appear in hunting scenes. Although indigenous in Egypt in large numbers during the Early Dynastic Period, they gradually became extinct. More early ivory is hippopotamus tooth than elephant tusk. Indeed, hippopotamus tooth is the hardest of the ivories and is extremely white. Whether rhinoceros horn was similarly used is uncertain. Later depictions of hippopotamus harpooning are ideological: the animal symbolises the chaos that was expelled by Pharaoh. Representations of the rhinoceros hunt are extremely rare, although Tuthmosis III once recalls killing one in Nubia.

The non-indigenous bear appears in New Kingdom Asian tribute scenes. A relief in the Luxor Temple shows a bear pursuing a Syrian fugitive up a tree (figure 42), an event mentioned also in a literary composition: 'Your name [reputation] is like that of Qasra-jadi, the Prince of Aser, when the bear found him in the balsam tree.' Clearly it was a popular story used as a model of derision.

Although the chase played an important role in Egyptian art, its function as a means of supplying food, at least in historical times, was minimal. It was chiefly a sport for the king and his magnates, but it had an underlying symbolism as an action protecting the world against the threat of disorder. Hunting particular animals, such as the hippopotamus and the lion, was a pharaonic prerogative, permitted only to the king's retainers by privilege. The royal hunt is attested by the traces of a wildlife park near the Soleb temple of Amenophis III in Nubia. An oval enclosure, measuring approximately 300 by 600 metres (1000 by 2000 feet), with an opening at one of the small sides, was surrounded by a net fence hanging from a cord suspended from forked sticks. These poles were placed in stone supports, and it is the latter that have been discovered. What happened can be gauged from tomb representations. Game was driven through the opening and roamed freely within the corral until shot by hunters operating from behind barriers (figure 5), or lassoed if required alive.

42. A bear, climbing up a tree in a wood outside a Syrian fortress, bites a fugitive in the leg. From the Luxor Temple, *temp*. Ramesses II, Nineteenth Dynasty. (After Wreszinski, *Atlas*, II, 1923-38, plate 66.)

Several kinds of animals were held in captivity to supply the offerings, which were subsequently consumed. Attempts to domesticate some species during the Old Kingdom were doomed to failure by the innate characteristics of the animals. Antelopes and gazelles, for instance, are too nervous to breed in confinement and, unlike cattle, do not live in herds based on hierarchic dominance, so refuse to accept man as their master. Whereas cows meekly follow the herdsmen in sacrificial processions, antelopes and gazelles had to be pushed and dragged.

Young gazelles could be tamed and are shown under the chair in a few tomb scenes, one pet even being buried in a coffin in the Valley of the Kings. Attempts at domestication were later abandoned as it was more satisfactory to trap these creatures in their natural habitat of the semi-desert adjacent to the Nile valley. Their presence here is confirmed by a New Kingdom prayer stating that Amun will be praised when he rescues the country from a disaster by 'the herdsmen in the field, the washermen on the riverbank, the gazelles upon the desert'.

Semi-domesticated ruminants appear in several Old Kingdom tomb scenes, such as that of Mereruka (figure 43, upper register), where five different species, mainly distinguished by the shape of their horns, are eating from mangers. At the rear of the row is a Dorcas gazelle, before it an ibex, and then probably an addax, preceded by an antelope, the foremost being an oryx. Although their names are denoted above in hieroglyphs, these are insufficient for definite identification. Moreover, as when drawing birds, the Egyptians are not always reliable in their zoological details.

Captured animals still occur in later offering processions. In a Nineteenth Dynasty letter a servant reports to his master that he has received his message: 'Give fodder to the oryxes and to the gazelles.' Whether they were kept in a temple or on a private estate is uncertain.

Gazelles are famed for their speed. A fine New Kingdom love poem places the following verses in the mouth of a maiden: 'Oh, that you come to your sister [beloved] swiftly, like a bounding gazelle in the desert. Its feet reel, its limbs are weary, terror has entered its body. A hunter pursues it with his hounds but they do not see it in its dust.' So the girl longs for her lover to run into her arms.

Antelopes, gazelles, ibexes and oryxes were housed in stables with scant room to manoeuvre. They were sometimes force-fed to improve the quality of their meat. Such was also the case with hyenas (figure 43, lower register), which were even thrown upon their backs in order to have their mouths stuffed, especially with ducks. The striped hyena was used for offerings but also trained

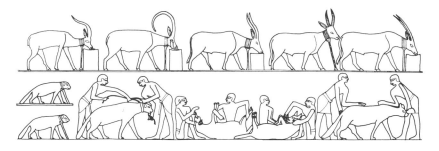

43. Upper register: antelopes eating from mangers. Lower register: force-feeding hyenas. From Saqqara, Sixth Dynasty. (After Duell *et.al.*, *The Mastaba of Mereruka*, II, 1938, plate 153.)

for hunting. Here, too, attempts at domestication failed and in the New Kingdom the animal became rare.

A famous representation of a hyena from the Eighteenth Dynasty Theban tomb of Amenemhat (TT 85) shows how this official encountered it in Syria and beat it on the head with a stick. A real event is depicted here, the intrepid officer wishing to boast of his cold-bloodedness.

That hyenas were already becoming scarce in the Old Kingdom is evidenced by a Memphite scene in which the tomb owner had two figures of hyenas altered to depict an antelope and a calf. Sufficient outline survives to confirm the original drawing. Elsewhere in the tomb the hyena is still represented for it belonged to the artistic canon, which gradually became divorced from reality.

The most exotic creatures feature in Nubian tribute scenes and texts (figure 44). Apart from the lion (see chapter 3) and monkeys and baboons (see chapter 4), they contain leopards, cheetahs, giraffes, and ostriches. Ostriches were neither domesticated nor eaten, but their feathers were ideal for fans. The eggs were even exported to Crete.

Leopards and cheetahs can be distinguished by their markings, the former having rosette-shaped spots whilst the latter have massive black blots. Moreover, the cheetah, the greyhound of the cats, is more slender (figure 49), its diagnostic characteristic being a black stripe from eye to mouth. The Egyptians used the same word for both, usually rendered (biologically incorrectly) as 'panther', with additional adjectives for differentiation. Nor were Egyptian artists always consistent regarding their anatomical

44. Nubian tribute bearers with a cheetah, giraffe, monkey, baboon and leopard. From the Theban tomb of Rekhmire (TT 100), Eighteenth Dynasty. (After Davies, *The Tomb of Rekh-mi-Rē at Thebes*, II, 1943, plates 17, 19, and 20.)

45. Green schist elephant-shaped palette with bone eyes. Purchased in Upper Egypt, Predynastic. (D 1162. Courtesy of the Musée d'art et d'histoire, Geneva.)

details, so it may be difficult to distinguish between them. In Hatshepsut's Deir el-Bahri temple both are clearly portrayed, the cheetahs carrying their heads erect, the leopards carrying theirs forward and slightly bowed. The texts and the 'tear-stripe' of the cheetahs provide further confirmation. Both animals, the booty of a southern expedition, are led on leashes by soldiers. Indeed, the cheetah, the swiftest animal on earth, could be tamed and was used like a hound. The skin of both animals was employed for priestly dress, that of the leopard being more highly valued.

Although the giraffe existed in prehistoric Egypt, as confirmed by rock drawings, it soon disappeared and became a conspicuous African import. Its skin was used for covers, its tail hair for wigs and for bands reputed to possess magical powers. Its extraordinary silhouette led to the use of the figure in the verb 'to foretell'. Primarily, it was appreciated as an astonishing creature.

The elephant also died out very early in Egyptian history, although somewhat later than the giraffe (figure 45). The demand for its ivory continued, the southernmost city of Egypt, where the material entered the country, aptly being called Elephantine. Its name in Egyptian (*Abu*) indicates both ivory and the animal. The tusk constitutes a very common hieroglyphic sign, used in writing various words.

During the New Kingdom elephant hunts are recorded from Syria, a country once described as 'rich in lions, panthers and bears', that is, in exotic beasts. Although the Syrian elephant is smaller than the African species, its diminutive size in a booty scene is clearly exaggerated.

The Eighteenth Dynasty pharaohs were wont to engage in such activities during their military campaigns, as described in the biography of the same Amenemhat who met the hyena. He relates that on a march, near the river Orontes: 'The king (Tuthmosis III) hunted 120 elephants for their tusks. I attacked the largest elephant among them, which charged against His Majesty, and cut off its hand (trunk), while it was alive, before the eyes of His Majesty, while I was standing in the water between two rocks.' This valiant deed resulted in Amenemhat being rewarded with gold and other valuables.

The ancient Egyptians were unacquainted with the circus or the travelling menagerie of the nineteenth century (figure 46). The wonders of remarkable creatures were thus mainly reserved for the pharaoh, who, already in the Old Kingdom, collected them to enrich his palace (figure 47). Tuthmosis III, lover of exotica,

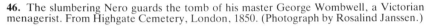

46. The slumbering Nero guards the tomb of his master George Wombwell, a Victorian menagerist. From Highgate Cemetery, London, 1850. (Photograph by Rosalind Janssen.)

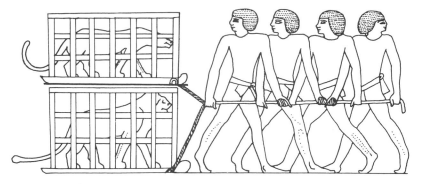

47. A leopard (above) and a lion (below), each in a strong cage, being drawn along on sledges. From the mastaba of Ptahhotep at Saqqara, Fifth Dynasty. (After Wreszinski, *Atlas*, III, 1923-38, plate 18.)

decorated a few rooms behind his festival hall at Karnak with scenes displaying numerous plants, supposedly gathered during his frequent Syrian enterprises. Depicted among the 275 floral specimens in this 'botanical garden' are 52 animals, primarily birds, but also cattle and a gazelle.

The Amarna Period is renowned for its love of nature. The North Palace at Amarna contained, in addition to the bird pond (see chapter 7), a yard housing antelopes and ibexes. They are carved in relief on the mangers running along its walls, with stone tethering rings in between.

A block from the Aten Temple at Karnak shows a villa in front of which are two round cages with cupola-shaped roofs. In each cage a lion is confined which could be viewed from a balcony approached by stairs. (It is thus reminiscent of the bear pits at Berne.) Behind the mansion, in a compound with trees, rove gazelles which can feed from a trough in one corner.

Excavations at the palace of Pi-Ramesses, the later New Kingdom Delta capital, have revealed the remains of one large elephant and parts of a lion in addition to antelope and gazelle bones. Although not quite a modern zoo, this comes close to King Henry I's wildlife park at Woodstock, Oxfordshire, where he kept his menagerie of lions, leopards, lynxes, camels and a favourite porcupine. The distance in outlook between this medieval English king and the Egyptian pharaohs thus appears to be negligible. Both display the same passion for exotic fauna.

9
Animals in human attitudes

Animals feature on all manner of household articles such as furniture, vessels, and toilette objects. Numerous beds and chairs rest on lions' and bulls' feet (figures 14 and 15), while the legs of folding stools are frequently carved as ducks' heads. Vessels were fashioned as ducks, fish or monkeys. Cosmetic boxes, particularly, assume the shape of ducks, a variant being a swimming girl holding the bird on her outstretched arms. Toilette implements take the form of various animals (figures 33, 37, 49) or are adorned with them (figures 24 and 32).

The lute, a musical instrument favoured by lovers and prostitutes, could carry a turned-back duck's head (figure 48), for, like cats and monkeys on utensils (figures 9 and 13), ducks' heads express eroticism. The symbolism of an ivory whip-handle, now in the Metropolitan Museum, New York, carved in the form of a galloping horse, is similarly obvious. Vessels adorned with goat-figured handles or projecting rams' heads (figure 24) have less obvious connotations, as do the pieces with jackals' and hounds' heads from a popular board-game, since the rules of play are unknown.

Very common are drawings of various animals in human attitudes: walking upright and using their forelegs as human limbs, sometimes even dressed. A Predynastic slate palette from Hierakonpolis, now in Oxford, depicts several animals and some monstrous creatures. On the back, in idyllic peace, lions and gazelles are kissing and a jackal plays the flute.

Amarna has yielded many small limestone figures, including a boat rowed by monkeys, a monkey harpist and a tensed monkey charioteer driving a monkey horse which is restrained by a monkey dwarf as groom. Possibly this is a parody on the well known scenes in which Akhenaten, standing at ease in his state chariot, drives his team with masterful dexterity. A satirical interpretation remains doubtful, however, and was certainly never intended in the majority of animal scenes on papyri and ostraca.

The most frequently depicted is the war between cats and mice, a motif also found in Persian, Indian, Arabic and Greek tales, and down to modern times (Tom and Jerry). The story refers to the natural hostility between these protagonists, portraying them as warriors, shooting arrows and storming fortresses. The course

48. (Right) Wooden spoon with openwork handle depicting a girl in a duck-headed boat playing a lute with a turned-back duck's head on the neck. From Sedment, Eighteenth Dynasty. (UC 14365.)

49. (Below) Bronze toilette implement in the form of a sprinting spotted cheetah, its back legs terminating in a papyrus umbel knife; unprovenanced, Eighteenth Dynasty. (UC 30134.)

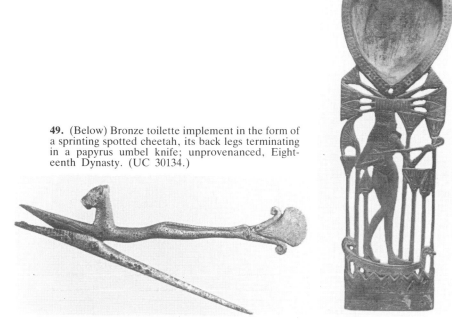

of events is unknown, since the sources are merely pictorial. It was clearly a folk-tale, transmitted from generation to generation, but never written down. Later parallels suggest that the war ended in a victory by the cats, thus restoring the natural order.

Other frequently occurring scenes depict cats serving a lady mouse with food and in attendance at their mistress's toilette. Animals play board-games and a hippopotamus brews beer, for which strenuous task he is aptly built. Sketches of animals as dancers or musicians, particularly monkeys, are popular. The girl on an ostracon (figure 50) is a later, less carefully executed, addition. Monkeys did indeed dance and were even trained to do so, but a donkey playing the harp, a crocodile playing the lute and a lion singing while strumming the lyre appear totally unrealistic.

Such drawings all illustrate unknown tales. Mockery may be involved in some instances, as in a drawing of a leopard biting a lion's paw. Above the lion is written 'King', and there is a word for leopard homophonous with one for 'Queen'. Is this a veiled reference to a harem intrigue? However, a scene of a crow ascending a ladder leaning against a fig-tree, in which a hippopotamus is gathering fruit, can hardly be a parody. It represents a topsy-turvy world, the reversal of natural order, a theme encountered likewise in the official literature. Another instance may be that of a youth punished by a cat-servant by order of a mouse-judge (figure 51).

All these depict animal tales as opposed to fables, which have a didactic purpose that is absent here. Yet fables, too, were known. They occur in a mythological story preserved in a Leiden papyrus from the Roman Period. However, a New Kingdom painted ostracon (figure 52) attests to a far earlier origin. The narrative relates how the feline goddess Tefnut quarrelled with her father Re, and became so incensed that she withdrew to the Nubian desert. Since Re sorely missed her, he dispatched the baboon-god Thoth to retrieve her. In the course of lengthy debates with Tefnut, he told her several fables containing moral lessons. The ostracon shows the baboon conversing with the cat, while one of the fables is alluded to above them by a vulture defending her eggs.

Famous among these stories is the *Tale of the Lion in Search of Man*, which also occurs in Aesop's *Fables*. A mighty lion, wandering through the desert, encountered a leopard whose skin was torn and who was half dead because of his wounds. When the lion asked him how he got into this condition, the leopard answered: 'It was man.' The lion said to him: 'Man, who is that?' The leopard replied: 'There is no one more cunning than man. May you not fall into his hands.' So the lion became enraged against man and went off in search of him.

Thereafter the lion met other animals which had likewise suffered through man, and he became more and more determined to find him. Once during his wanderings a tiny mouse strayed into his paws. When the lion was about to crush him, the mouse said: 'Don't crush me, my Lord. If you eat me you'll not be sated. If you grant me the breath of life, I'll once grant you your own breath of life. I'll let you escape your misfortune.' The lion laughed incredulously, but he gave in and let the mouse run away.

Now it happened that a hunter with a net set traps and dug a pit for the lion, and the lion fell into the pit. The hunter put him into the net and bound him with leather straps. So the lion lay suffering in the desert. Thereupon Fate wished to make his joke

50. Limestone figured ostracon showing a young girl dancing while a monkey plays the double oboe. From Deir el-Medina, West Thebes, New Kingdom. (E 25309. Courtesy of the Musée du Louvre, Paris.)

51. (Below) Painted limestone ostracon showing a mouse-judge and a cat-servant chastising a pleading youth. From West Thebes, Nineteenth Dynasty. (OI 13951. Courtesy of the Oriental Institute of the University of Chicago.)

come true, because the lion had boasted that he could catch man, and she made the little mouse come and stand before the lion. And the mouse asked: 'Do you recognise me? You once granted me my breath of life, now I come to repay you for it and rescue you from your misfortune. It is fine to return good to him who did it to you.' And the mouse set its teeth to the bonds that bound the lion and gnawed through the straps. After he had so released the lion, he hid in his mane and went off with him to the mountain on that day.

Animals also speak in Egyptian literary compositions, in which they usually help man. In the *Tale of the Two Brothers* cows warn the younger brother that the elder is anxious to kill him, wrongly believing that he has deceived him with his wife. In the *Book of the Dead* the deceased declares that he has heard 'every word that the donkey exchanged with the cat'. This is an allusion to an unknown myth, the cat being Re, the donkey the god Seth.

Thus the hierarchy of life was less accentuated than in modern experience. Animals were regarded as individuals, a species like a nation. Hence the Egyptian language contained no generic word for 'animal'. They were simply too familiar. Daily contact with household animals, using and admiring, even loving them, constituted an integral part of the ancient Egyptians' existence.

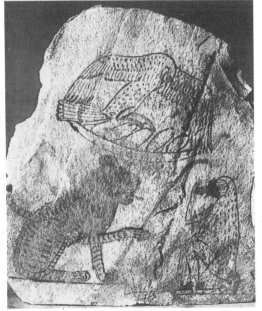

52. Painted limestone ostracon showing a baboon (Thoth) conversing with a cat (Tefnut); above, a vulture protecting its eggs. From Deir el-Medina, West Thebes, Twentieth Dynasty. (Ägyptisches Museum 21443. Courtesy of the Staatliche Museen zu Berlin, German Democratic Republic.)

10
Further reading

The following select bibliography has been compiled from the wealth of available material. Further literature on individual animals is to be found in the *Lexikon der Ägyptologie*, six volumes, Wiesbaden, 1972-86.

Boessneck, J. *Die Haustiere in Altägypten*. Veröffentlichungen der zoologischen Staatssammlung München 3. Munich, 1953.

Brunner-Traut, E. *Altägyptische Tiergeschichte und Fabel. Gestalt und Strahlkraft*. Darmstadt, 1968.

Brunner-Traut, E. *Die Alten Ägypter. Verborgenes Leben unter Pharaonen*. Stuttgart, 1974.

Clutton-Brock, J. *Domestic Animals from Early Times*. British Museum (Natural History), London, 1981.

Dorst, J. and Dandelot, P. *A Field Guide to the Larger Mammals of Africa*. London, 1972.

Handoussa, T. 'Le chien d'agrément en Ancienne Egypte', *Göttinger Miszellen*, 89 (1986), 23-41.

Hornung, E. 'Die Bedeutung des Tieres im Alten Ägypten', *Studium Generale*, 20 (1967), 69-84.

Houlihan, P. F. *The Birds of Ancient Egypt*. Warminster, 1986.

Montet, P. 'Les boeufs égyptiens', *Kêmi*, 13 (1952), 43-58.

Nibbi, A. 'Some Remarks on Ass and Horse in Ancient Egypt and the Absence of the Mule', *Zeitschrift für ägyptische Sprache und Altertumskunde*, 106 (1979), 148-68.

Paton, D. *Animals of Ancient Egypt: Materials for a 'Sign List' of Egyptian Hieroglyphs*. Princeton, 1925.

Vandier d'Abbadie, J. 'Les singes familiers dans l'Ancienne Egypte. 'I. L'Ancien Empire', *Revue d'Egyptologie*, 16 (1964), 147-77. 'II. Le Moyen Empire', *Revue d'Egyptologie*, 17 (1965), 177-88. 'III. Le Nouvel Empire', *Revue d'Egyptologie*, 18 (1966), 143-201.

11
Museums to visit

As all museums with an Egyptology collection have objects portraying animals only major museums in Britain and Ireland are listed here. Intending visitors are advised to ascertain the times of opening before making a special journey.

Ashmolean Museum of Art and Archaeology, Beaumont Street, Oxford OX1 2PH. Telephone: 0865 278000.

Birmingham Museum and Art Gallery, Chamberlain Square, Birmingham B3 3DH. Telephone: 021-235 2834.

Bolton Museum and Art Gallery, Le Mans Crescent, Bolton, Lancashire BL1 1SE. Telephone: 0204 22311 extension 2191.

British Museum, Great Russell Street, London WC1B 3DG. Telephone: 01-636 1555.

City of Bristol Museum and Art Gallery, Queens Road, Bristol, Avon BS8 1RL. Telephone: 0272 299771.

Dundee Art Galleries and Museums, Albert Square, Dundee, Angus DD1 1DA. Telephone: 0382 23141.

Durham University Oriental Museum, Elvet Hill, Durham DH1 3TH. Telephone: 091 3742911.

Fitzwilliam Museum, Trumpington Street, Cambridge CB2 1RB. Telephone: 0223 332900.

Glasgow Art Gallery and Museum, Kelvingrove, Glasgow G3 8AG. Telephone: 041-357 3929.

Hunterian Museum, The University of Glasgow, Glasgow G12 8QQ. Telephone: 041-330 4221.

Leicestershire Museum and Art Gallery, 96 New Walk, Leicester LE1 6TD. Telephone: 0533 554100.

Liverpool Museum, William Brown Street, Liverpool L3 8EN. Telephone: 051-207 0001 or 5451.

Manchester Museum, The University of Manchester, Oxford Road, Manchester M13 9PL. Telephone: 061-273 3333.

National Museum of Ireland, Kildare Street, Dublin 2. Telephone: 01-765521.

Petrie Museum of Egyptian Archaeology, University College London, Gower Street, London WC1E 6BT. Telephone: 01-387 7050 extension 2884.

Plymouth City Museum and Art Gallery, Drake Circus, Plymouth, Devon PL4 8AJ. Telephone: 0752 668000 extension 4878.

Royal Museum of Scotland, Chambers Street, Edinburgh EH1
1JF. Telephone: 031-225 7534.
Sheffield City Museum, Weston Park, Sheffield, South Yorkshire
S10 2TP. Telephone: 0742 768588.
Swansea Museum, Victoria Road, Swansea, West Glamorgan
SA1 1SN. Telephone: 0792 53763.
Ulster Museum, Botanic Gardens, Belfast, Northern Ireland BT9
5AB. Telephone: 0232 381251-6.

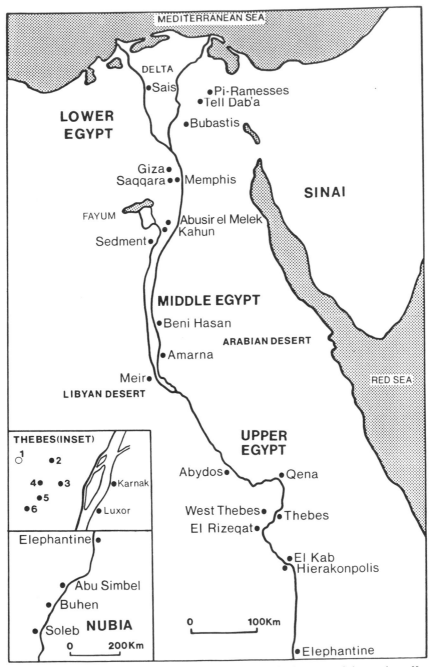

53. Map of ancient Egypt, showing the sites mentioned in the text and the captions. Key to inset of Thebes: 1, Valley of the Kings; 2, Deir el-Bahri; 3, Ramesseum; 4, Deir el-Medina; 5, Medinet Habu; 6, Malkata.

Index

Page numbers in italic refer to illustrations. The index does not include the names of those animals which form the main subject matter of individual chapters.